ESSENTIAL **DK** COMPUTERS

INTERNET

ENHANCING
YOUR WEBSITE

About This Book

Enhancing Your Website is an easy-to-follow guide to improving the effectiveness of a basic website: the next step after building pages with an HTML editor, such as Microsoft Frontpage 2000.

HIS BOOK EXPLAINS HOW TO CREATE A successful website, from assembling web pages in usable structures to editing the code of the page in raw HTML. Ideal if you have experimented with web pages or created a basic website and wish to adopt the techniques of professional website construction, each chapter deals with a different aspect of production and builds on previous explanations so that your knowledge develops gradually.

The themes of the book include how to design considerably for your visitors' needs, how to recognize and work with different elements inside a web page, and how to promote your site once you have developed it. At each stage, potential problems are identified and explained, so that troubleshooting is made easy.

The chapters and the subsections present the information using step-by-step

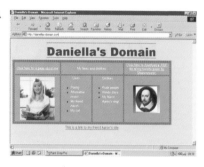

sequences. Virtually every step is accompanied by an illustration showing how your screen should look at each stage.

The book contains several features to help you understand both what is happening and what you need to do.

Command keys, such as ENTER and CTRL, are shown in these rectangles: Enter↵ and Ctrl, so that there's no confusion, for example, over whether you should press that key or type the letters "ctrl."

Cross-references are shown in the text as left- or right-hand page icons: ⟦ and ⟧. The page number and the reference are shown at the foot of the page.

As well as the step-by-step sections, there are boxes that explain a feature in detail, and tip boxes that provide alternative methods. Finally, at the back, you will find a glossary of common terms, and a comprehensive index.

ESSENTIAL **DK** COMPUTERS

INTERNET

ENHANCING YOUR WEBSITE

ANN LIGHT & DES WATSON

A Dorling Kindersley Book

Dorling Kindersley
LONDON, NEW YORK, SYDNEY, DELHI,
PARIS, MUNICH, and JOHANNESBURG

Produced for Dorling Kindersley Limited by
Design Revolution, Queens Park Villa,
30 West Drive, Brighton, East Sussex BN2 2GE

EDITORIAL DIRECTOR Ian Whitelaw
SENIOR DESIGNER Andy Ashdown
PROJECT EDITOR John Watson
DESIGNERS Paul Bowler and Andrew Easton

SENIOR EDITOR Mary Lindsay
SENIOR MANAGING ART EDITOR Nigel Duffield
DTP DESIGNER Jason Little
PRODUCTION CONTROLLER Michelle Thomas

Published in Great Britain in 2000 by
Dorling Kindersley Limited,
9 Henrietta Street, London WC2E 8PS

2 4 6 8 10 9 7 5 3 1

A CIP catalog record for this book is available from the British Library.

ISBN 0-7513-1301-7

Color reproduced by First Impressions, London
Printed in Italy by Graphicom

For our complete
catalog visit
www.dk.com

CONTENTS

CONSIDERATIONS

A successful site is one that visitors like to visit. You can attract them with interesting content, but to keep them visiting and returning, there are many little details that make a difference.

PLANNING YOUR SITE

A website, consisting of one or more web pages, is merely a way of structuring information on the web to make it more meaningful, coherent, and accessible. Think of websites as the basic conceptual unit that makes up the web.

THE VALUE OF STYLE

● Even one page showing a single line of text can be a website. At their most complex, websites can be an impressive marketing device where style as well as content helps to communicate your message to your visitors. It is not a matter of size, but of understanding how to use the web for your own ends.

Many sites include a site map showing the structure of the pages within the site.

QUESTIONS TO ASK YOURSELF WHEN DEVELOPING YOUR SITE

1 Why am I developing this site?
2 Who do I want to visit it?
3 What visitor response do I want?
4 What messages do I want to convey?
5 What traits do my visitors share?
6 Do they have particular requirements?
7 Do they need to contact me?
8 Do they need contact links?
9 Should I include my contact details?
10 What should I add to the site next?
11 Is the site's structure flexible?
12 How often will the site be updated?

GETTING INSPIRATION FROM OTHER PEOPLE'S SITES

Once you have decided what you wish to achieve with your site, you might want to look at how other people and organizations have met a similar challenge. Sites are built for many reasons: to be promotional, informative, funny, to sell merchandise or services, or to locate like-minded people. Find several sites built by developers with similar aims to your own and explore how they have approached the design and structure of each site. The web was conceived as a tool for sharing information across the globe, and this goes for good design ideas too.

ARRANGEMENT

● There are two ways that you can benefit from looking at others' work. One way is to look at sites with your browser and think about their arrangement. You might wish to explore the sites in terms of the categories shown in the next few pages.

An invaluable resource
Websites are posted on the web to be read and used. However, they are also all available as sources of information and ideas about how you can improve your own site.

OTHER BENEFITS

The other way to benefit is to look at how these effects were achieved, for example, by examining the instruc-tions to the browser about what to display. This is not as complex as it sounds, and in the following chapters you will be shown how to find, read, and make sense of the code that instructs the browser ⬒.

Establishing a Website's Boundaries

You can usually tell by looking when you have moved from one website to another by following a link. But it is very different from picking up a new book. The web is a sea of pages, each of which can be accessed by using the same form of request, regardless of who manufactured it or where it is stored. The browser shows pages from every web server in the same way. Boundaries have to be manufactured.

There is a balance to be struck between following the conventions that have grown up on the web and developing your own style. Consistency in how certain functions are presented across all websites gives the web a familiarity that helps people who are still learning to use the web. However, website developers also create their own codes to use within a website to give visitors some sense of the site's identity.

CONSISTENCY ACROSS THE WEB

● Most links in the text on web pages are colored blue, and underlined, when you first see them. This shows that they are hot. Once you have visited a link, and return to the original page from which you visited it, you will find that the link has changed color.

● This system of coloring helps people to recognize links in the text, and also to know where they have been. Many developers follow this convention.

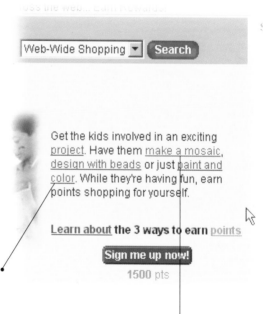

The blue links tell you that they have not been visited.

This link has already been visited, and this is indicated by the purple coloring of the text.

CONSISTENCY ACROSS YOUR SITE

● You may want to follow the color code for links, but you will want to develop consistency that is particular to your site to make it distinct from others. The use of a logo on each page, the same fonts and heading styles, colors and backgrounds, and using the same navigation devices all reinforce the identity of pages belonging together. In this way you can claim your territory.

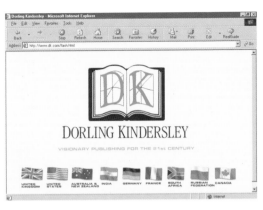

WAYS THAT VISITORS APPROACH WEBSITES

● Some visitors will use the URL of your introductory page to approach your site. But others may not arrive at your introductory page first. They may have found your site by chance, by using a search engine that has noted a particularly relevant page. It is therefore good promotional practice to mark every page with orientating information, such as what the site is and the range of what it offers.

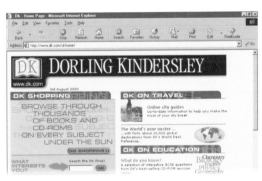

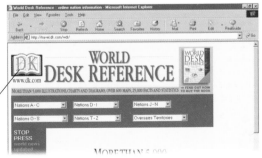

The DK logo on every page provides a link straight back to the homepage.

Keeping Things Simple

There are differences in the technology that your visitors will be using to look at your site. A site that is rich in complicated features needs to justify their use. Slow modem speeds and old versions of browsers will not do justice to a technically complex site. Old software could turn your rich design into clutter.

PICTURES

● Images are attractive, but they slow down the site's arrival. A detailed picture will be useful if you want someone to recognize you from your web page, show off your new baby, or display unusual merchandise. But a simpler image will be appropriate, for example, when using an image to create atmosphere or to give directions with a map. If you specify the dimensions of your image, you allow the text to appear on the page before the picture, which gives the visitor something to read.

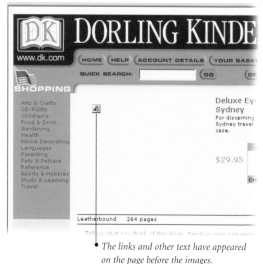

The links and other text have appeared on the page before the images.

FRAMES

● Some pages are divided into separate sections that can be scrolled through independently, or stay static as other parts move. Not all visitors will be able to view frames with their browser. Many sites offer **frames** or **without frames** options.

This site uses frames.

PLUG-INS

● These allow you to run extra functions on the site, such as audio, animation, and video, but many visitors will not have the software on their computer to use that section of your site. It is also possible that they may not wish to download it immediately either. If you use these functions, offer a link to download the plug-in.

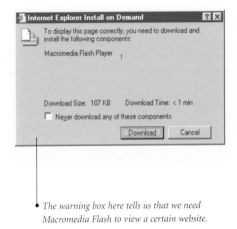

● *The warning box here tells us that we need Macromedia Flash to view a certain website.*

NAVIGATION AROUND YOUR SITE

● Your site is more than a series of pages. It is an aid for your visitors to locate information. But if this information is hidden behind links that are slow to connect, it is important to label all text links and buttons clearly. This sounds simple, but care must be taken that the links and buttons are allocated to the correct categories of information. Check your categories with colleagues to see if they would allocate the same items to the same categories as you would. It is more important to be clear than to be clever.

● *The links here are well labeled and easy to understand.*

STRUCTURING YOUR SITE

There are many ways to structure your site using linking patterns to help your visitors navigate. Here are three possible structure shapes that can either be used alone or combined, depending on the characteristics of your site.

HIERARCHICAL
● This is useful for displaying large amounts of information, provided that your visitors can determine which section to search in. In this structure, pages are linked in a branching arrangement that allows increasingly precise definitions. **Yahoo.com** is an excellent example of a hierarchical structure.

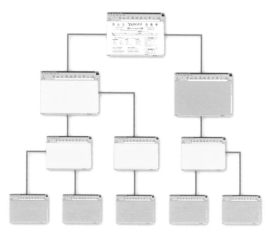

NETWORK
● A network connects all the pages by providing links top and bottom. Many different functions can be combined with this structure, and visitors can browse easily. Using frames can be an effective way of building a network, putting page choices in a small frame that stays static and displaying the results in the main frame.

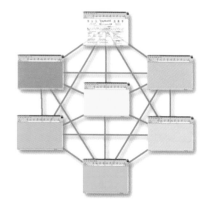

LINEAR

● If you want to take your visitors through a sequence in the order of your choice, a linear structure is useful. Links are labeled **Next** and **Back** and only offer visitors one new page at a time. A linear structure is useful for some educational materials and for getting information from your visitors in forms.

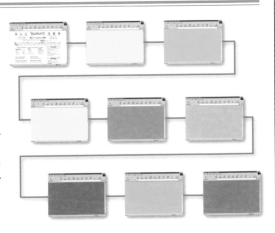

COMBINATION

● There is no need to stick strictly to one kind of structure. Hierarchies may produce lists of categories, which are not very eye-catching. Networks require that each page lists every possible link, which can be space-hungry. A combination may therefore be the answer. However, the navigation tools must be made obvious. So if you put your list of internal links on the top left-hand side of the page, put the same links at the bottom of the page as well. Make sure that you refer to the same links in the same way each time, so that your visitors know if they have already seen those pages or if there is something new for them to see.

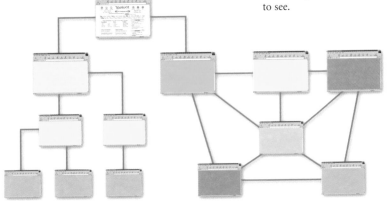

MAINTAINING YOUR SITE

Sites do not need much attention, unless you have external links, regularly updated material, or a feedback form. Site maintenance, when it is required, needs attention paid to when and how it is to be done while bearing your visitors in mind.

LINKS

● It is important to check your external links regularly and alter them if they are no longer connecting to anything. It is possible to download a small program that you can install to notify you of broken links.

Not Found

The requested URL /foo.html was not found on

Apache/1.3.6 Server at www.cogs.susx.ac.uk

UNDER CONSTRUCTION

● Some sites have empty pages linked to their menu pages that the developer intends to fill soon. If you have not finished a page, but wish to link it to your main index, put a note with the link, explaining that the page is not completed. This saves visitors following useless links, while giving them an indication of what will one day be there. If you know when it will be completed, you could also put a date for completion – but stick to it.

Site under construction
Please come back soon

REDESIGNING YOUR SITE

A year of real time is seven years on the web. Websites are redesigned frequently to keep them up-to-date. Redesigns work best when visitors can tell it is the same site, and can find their way around. Be radical, but continue to be helpful.

UPDATING YOUR SITE

● Updating your site keeps it interesting. If you intend to update regularly, tell your visitors when to expect the new material either by explaining this on the site, or by collecting visitors' email addresses and send them an email telling them of the changes. Keep to your plans if you publicize an update.

Press. Reporting

As DK focuses on follows:

DK will be publish Adventure, Seem Funhouse. DK wil season in the no

● *The panel here allows the viewer to read about any updates or news to the site.*

KEEP OLD MATERIAL

● If you are adding new material to your site, it will be tempting to do so by removing old pages or changing their contents. But taking away old material means that your visitors may not be able to find what it was that impressed them about your site. If you move material, direct your visitors to its new location, for instance, an archive.

News archive - June 2000

News archive - May 2000

News archive - April 2000

News archive - March 2000

FEEDBACK

● It has become a courtesy on the web that whoever asks a question will get an answer, and the response will be swift. If you ask for comments or contributions on your site, monitor your incoming messages and respond to them.

We really want your feedback -- which you can send using the easy form below, or e-mail da@nd.co

Comment:

Your e-mail address:

INSIDE A WEBSITE

It is important to know something about the components that make up a website, and how they can be combined to produce an effective whole.

COMPONENTS OF A WEBSITE

Websites achieve their effects by assembling components, such as photos, graphics, tables, and text, in specified ways over several pages. This chapter takes a look at what your visitors see and how to link pages together for maximum effect.

LINK BUTTON

Here is a link to another web page. Links are described further on page 18.

...described further on page 18.

TEXT TO BE ENTERED BY THE USER

This is an area of the screen where the user can type in text – the appropriate box is selected by the user (usually by means of a mouse click); the user types in some appropriate text, and on clicking the corresponding GO button, the text that has been input is sent to the computer serving the page; the GO button is another link.

MULTIMEDIA LINKS

Other web pages contain links to data in a variety of multimedia formats. For example, video, audio files, and animations, among others, can be loaded and played on the user's computer. It must be borne in mind, however, that some visitors will not have the necessary software to play everything.

HEAD TEXT

Online city guides

The page contains some simple text – displayed in different colors and fonts. Head text must be used consistently in the web pages.

BODY TEXT

Up-to-date information to help most of your city break.

Some web pages consist of little more than simple text. Sites that concentrate heavily on information that is conveyed verbally make the best use of simple text. A light-hearted personal website would not attract many visitors if its content consisted only of simple text.

IMAGES

The page contains some images – the HTML definition of the page includes commands to tell the browser to load specific image files and display them at particular locations on the screen.

LINKS

Links are most useful when they come with a short description of what is behind them; this stops visitors from wasting time by downloading pages they do not require.

There are three possible kinds of links to introduce into the pages of a website, and in well-designed sites, it is clear to the visitor which one is which.

EXTERNAL LINKS

● Any link that connects one of your pages to part of another site is external. Identify your external links with details of the site being linked. Remember, though, that you have no control over what is exhibited on the page you have linked to, or whether it still exists. It is worth checking your external links regularly to ensure they stay valid. Some site developers place a disclaimer with external links to point out to visitors that they are not responsible for the content that follows.

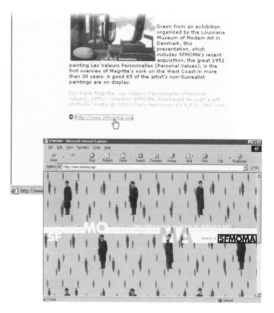

Drawn from an exhibition organized by the Louisiana Museum of Modern Art in Denmark, this presentation, which includes SFMOMA's recent acquisition, the great 1952 painting Les Valeurs Personnelles (Personal Values), is the first overview of Magritte's work on the West Coast in more than 30 years. A good 65 of the artist's non-Surrealist paintings are on display.

Pic: René Magritte, Les Valeurs Personnelles (Personal Values), 1952; Collection SFMOMA, Purchased through a gift of Phyllis Wattis © 2000 Charly Herscovici o/o A.R.S., New York

➔ http://www.sfmoma.org

WHAT DO LINKS LOOK LIKE?

Some links may be pieces of text leading to a page that develops the ideas being expressed. Some textual links are separate from the main business of the page: they have been made into headings for paragraphs that describe the link. Other links will be beside the text, or below it, and these may be incorporated into graphics, such as pictures or buttons. Remember that links in long passages of text may interrupt people as they read.

INTERNAL LINKS

● Any link that connects different pages together within your site is an internal link. These links can be used in many ways (see the section on structuring your site ⌐). Internal links require less maintenance. Once you have checked that they work, you do not need to re-examine them unless you change the pages in question or move the site to another location.

IN-PAGE LINKS

● It is possible to link to any part of a page, using the bookmark facilities of HTML ⌐. You can do this within a single page by placing bookmarks at key points and then linking to them. You might use this in a document that runs to several screens of material; the text can be divided into sections with subheadings, and these subheadings can be indexed at the top of the page with a series of links to the sections.

HTML

You may never have thought about how web pages create the effects that you see in your browser, but it is useful to understand these matters if you want to develop your site beyond the basics.

WHAT THE BROWSER SEES

In the last chapter, we explored the elements that make up the appearance of a website. But what the browser receives when a file is downloaded is a string of instructions about how to display the page. The instructions come as tags informing the browser how to show different parts of the page and where to find other, linked, files. There is a benefit in exploring the internal workings of the site if you want to move past the functions that your HTML editor can perform for you.

HTML COMMANDS

HTML files are downloaded by the user's web browser program (such as Microsoft Internet Explorer or Netscape Navigator), and the browser interprets the HTML commands contained in these files. These commands tell the browser what to display on the screen. The HTML files will nearly always contain text for display on the screen, but HTML is capable of much more powerful actions. Commands are available to format the text in specific ways, to include images and other multimedia objects, to support forms that the user can fill in, and to run programs. In this chapter, we look at some simple HTML and the next chapter shows you how you can use it.

HTML IS NOT:

• A way of giving precise control of the appearance of the document on the user's screen. Because HTML is intended to define the structure of the page, it is the job of the browser to decide how the HTML code is to be interpreted for the particular display.

• A word processing format. Quite apart from the lack of control over the document's final appearance, HTML is not nearly powerful enough to do the things that users now expect. Use a specialized tool such as Microsoft Word or LaTeX.

VIEWING THE HTML CODE

By presenting a URL to a web browser, a rendered version of the page appears on the screen. But nearly all web browsers offer the additional useful facility of being able to display the HTML source file downloaded from the server.

1 VIEWING THE WEB PAGE

● Open a web page in your browser window.
● Click on **View** and select **Source** from the drop-down menu.

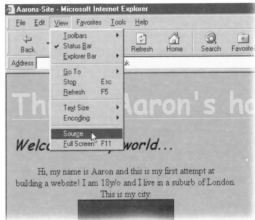

2 VIEWING THE HTML SOURCE

● Notepad will open and the HTML source code for the web page will appear in the window.

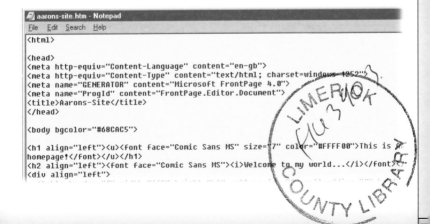

```
aarons-site.htm - Notepad
File Edit Search Help
<html>

<head>
<meta http-equiv="Content-Language" content="en-gb">
<meta http-equiv="Content-Type" content="text/html; charset=windows-1252">
<meta name="GENERATOR" content="Microsoft FrontPage 4.0">
<meta name="ProgId" content="FrontPage.Editor.Document">
<title>Aarons-Site</title>
</head>

<body bgcolor="#68CAC5">

<h1 align="left"><u><font face="Comic Sans MS" size="7" color="#FFFF00">This is
homepage!</font></u></h1>
<h2 align="left"><font face="Comic Sans MS"><i>Welcome to my world...</i></font>
<div align="left">
```

THE STRUCTURE OF THE PAGE

HTML tags control different aspects of the page. Originally, most tags were intended to give information about the structure of the page so that it could be viewed as a document of a recognizable shape by any browser. The actual appearance of the page was then determined by the browser's settings, which could be altered by users.

THE HTML TAG

Every web page starts by declaring that the tags on the page are written in HTML. At the end of the page, the corresponding tag is </html> to indicate that it is complete.

THE HEAD SECTION

```
<head>
<meta http-equiv="Content-Language"
<meta http-equiv="Content-Type" cont
<meta name="GENERATOR" content="Micr
<meta name="ProgId" content="FrontPa
<title>Aarons-Site</title>
</head>
```

The page is broken into two sections: Head and Body. The information in the head is not visible on the page, but the material between the <title> and </title> appears as the title of the page when opened in a browser.

TAGS		
Each HTML instruction that you use consists of a pair of tags, which	define the scope of the command. For example, <table> marks the	beginning of a table and </table> marks the end of the table.

LEFT ALIGN

```
<h1 align="left"><u><font face="C
homepage!</font></u></h1>
<h2 align="left"><font face="Comi
<div align="left">
```

These headings are explicitly defined to be aligned with the left-hand margin. This is, in fact, the default.

BODY

```
</head>

<body bgcolor="#68CAC5">

<h1 align="left"><u><font face="Con
```

The body of the page has certain characteristics. In the basic <body> tag on this page, some instructions have been added about the background color of the page: "#.. .. .."

... and this is my garden at home.

've recently started a garden design course at ge. Click here to see some of the designs in my project folder.

FORMATTING

```
<td width="751" height="46" alig
  <p align="center"><font size="
  first attempt at<br>
  building a website!
  I am 18y/o and I live in a sub
  </font><img border="1" src="lo
```

*There are tags that let you control the layout of the material on the page. If you write the text for a page in HTML, it will run on continuously filling lines on the user's screen unless you command it to break in certain places.
 introduces a new line in the text, whereas <p> introduces a line space for new paragraphs.*

CENTERED TEXT

```
<td width="751" height="46" a
  <p align="center"><font size
  first attempt at<br>
```

There are several ways in which text may be centered on the screen. Here, the center directive indicates that each line of the paragraph should be centered.

THE APPEARANCE OF TEXT

Gradually more appearance tags have been added to control appearance, but there are still differences in how they appear in different browsers. The "italic" tags have replaced "emphasis" tags. There are also font tags and ways of changing the color.

TEXT APPEARANCE

```
 size="7" color="#FFFF00">This is

>Welcome to my world...</i></font>

llspacing="0" cellpadding="0" bord
```

Your text will appear small and black unless you add some formatting. Text automatically appears aligned left. You can change many details of the appearance and more instructions are added with each new version of HTML.

HEADING SIZE

```
<h1 align="left"><u><font face="Con
homepage!</font></u></h1>
<h2 align="left"><font face="Comic
<div align="left">
  <table border="0" width="662" hei
    <tr>
```

<h1> </h1> controls the size of the heading. There are tags from <h1> to <h6>.

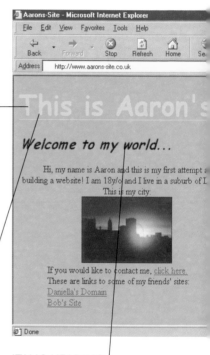

ITALIC HEADING

```
'7" color="#FFFF00">This is Aaron's

me to my world...</i></font></h2>

ing="0" cellpadding="0" bordercolor=
```

Text between <i> and </i> appears in an italic font.

COLOR

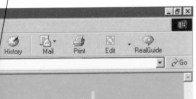

• *The color of the text may be specified.*

... and this is my garden at home.

we recently started a garden design course at
ege. Click here to see some of the designs in
my project folder.

ALIGNMENT

*<align=" right"> shifts the text to the right-hand
side of the page as it appears in the browser.*

FONTS

*There is a range of font names <font face="…"> ,
font sizes <size="…">, and colors
<color="#.. .. .."> to choose from.*

UNDERLINING

• *<u> </u> underlines the "text.*

TAGS WITHIN TAGS

Notice that tags nest other tags within
them. The writing that appears on the
screen is the material that sits between
the final opening tag that describes its
appearance and all the closing tags that
end the instructions.

SPECIAL CHARACTERS

HTML supports a wide
range of characters, but
not all of them appear on
the keyboard. For example,

the copyright symbol is
denoted in HTML as
©. Accented characters
are input using a similar

mechanism. For a full list
of these special characters,
consult the references at
the end of the book.

IMAGES AND LINKS

Images, graphics, email, and web links are all created by reference to a file elsewhere. These are simple to follow in the text if you regard them as an instruction and an address. Many errors creep in when calling other files, so spotting anomalies is useful.

IMAGES

```
I am 18y/o and I live in a suburb
</font><img border="1" src="londo
/td>
td width="431" height="46" align="
```

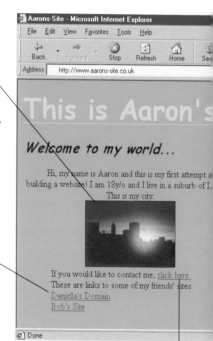

The images on a page are introduced by calling them with the <img src= "….."> tag. You do have to specify a source of an image or you will get a broken image. Details such as border width, image width, and height may also be added. Adding the dimensions of the image allows the page to download more quickly, and so is recommended.

LINKS

```
here.<br>
</a>These are links to some of my f
<a href="http://www.daniellas-domai
Bob's Site</a></td>
```

You can attach hypertext links to other pages using the same anchor <a> tag, sites, or in-page links by using <a href= "http://www. …."> your linked site here </a>. If the page is part of your own site, you will only need to give the file name of the page. The link displayed here is external.

EMAIL

```
51">
```

```
u would like to contact me, <a href="mailto:aaron@desrev.co.uk">click
```

You can include a link to someone's email by writing <a href="mailto: ….@….." Your name here </a>. This will make your name clickable so that an email box is displayed ready for a message.

TABLES, LISTS, AND FRAMES

There are further systems for structuring text that are useful to building pages. These include tables, which, as you will see, are a helpful device for structuring page elements, such as images, text, links, and lists, as well as straightforward data.

TABLES

```
<h2 align="left"><font Face="Comic Sans
<div align="left">
    <table border="0" width="662" height='
        <tr>
            <td width="751" height="46" align
                <p align="center"><font size="3
                first attempt at<br>
                building a website!
                I am 18y/o and I live in a subu
                </font><img border="1" src="lon
            </td>
            <td width="431" height="46" align
                and
                this is my garden at home.</fon
                <p><img border="0" src="garden.
            </td>
        </tr>
    </table>
</div>
```

This page shows how a table <table> looks in HTML. It is a simple table with one row <tr> and two cells <td>. You can see that images and text can be included in a table. In fact, any feature of HTML can be incorporated into a table and it is a useful structuring device.

LISTS AND FRAMES

HTML supports three forms of lists: ordered <col>, unordered <ul>, and definition lists <dl>.

The HTML <frame> tag allows you to write web pages that have the effect of splitting up the display screen into a set of independent frames, each of which displays a different document.

WORKING WITH HTML

Once you have become familiar with the internal workings of a website, you can start to use raw HTML code by importing and editing it from other websites that contain appealing features.

USING HTML TO ENHANCE YOUR SITE

When you see a new page of source code for the very first time, its appearance can be alarming; but once you understand what each section does, you will find that it starts to make sense. There are three reasons for coming to grips with how HTML works to create a web page. First, you can resolve problems with a page that you have built with an HTML editor, such as Frontpage. Second, you can use examples from other people's code to add to your site. Third, you will be able to update your site with newly invented tags. This means learning to recognize and use some basic HTML components. And there is no substitute for experimentation if you really want to learn about HTML.

THE PHILOSOPHY OF HTML

Beware - use HTML wisely! HTML was never designed to be used as a tool to specify the low-level appearance of a document. For example, details of fonts and their sizes, colors, and page layout should not really be specified in the HTML files – instead, this information should be specified separately in a style sheet. HTML is designed for document "markup" since it allows you to specify objects such as headings, paragraphs, lists, tables, and hypertext links.

In practice, of course, many web pages blatantly violate this rule. HTML does offer facilities for the low-level control of appearance and these facilities are used extensively. But there is an important motivation for observing this philosophy. When creating a web page, you should not make assumptions about the type of computer being used to view the page. As an extreme example, consider the effect of displaying a page designed for a large high-resolution color screen on the small monochrome LCD screen of a mobile phone.

USING SOURCE CODE

Having access to the source code of other web pages offers some key benefits:

● You can see how other people write HTML, and if you find a web page that incorporates an interesting characteristic, you can examine the HTML source code to see how it was done.

● Many HTML files will include a header identifying the package used in their creation. This may help you select the right HTML package for your needs.

● These HTML files can form the basis of your own pages – you may be able to extract ideas and even HTML code to include in your pages. The HTML source can be viewed and edited using a text editor or it can be input into an HTML editing package.

KEEPING YOUR CODE TIDY

If you are going to work with your source code, you will want it to be as easy to understand as possible. You may not have seen it before; it may be a long time before you look at it again – make sure that there is space between sections and that the different sections are indented neatly so that you can see where they begin and end. Ensure that beginning and their matching ending tags are vertically aligned. Many of the HTML-aware text editors will do this for you automatically.

```html
<html>
 <head>
 <title>Rainfall Table</title>
 </head>
 <body>
 <table border="1" width="60%" cellpadding="20">
  <caption>Recent rainfall in my garden</caption>
  <tr><th>Year</th><th>Rainfall</th></tr>
  <tr><td>1997</td><td>35.42</td></tr>
  <tr><td>1998</td><td>37.18</td></tr>
  <tr><td>1999</td><td>34.88</td></tr>
 </table>
 </body>
</html>
```

The beginning and end tags are aligned.

The product of the HTML code.

	Recent rainfall in my garden	
Year	Rainfall	
1997	35.42	
1998	37.18	
1999	34.88	

IMPORTING HTML

If you want to work with the raw HTML of a site – either your own, or someone else's – you will want to import the page files into a text editor. Though you have seen how to view source code in your browser, you cannot edit it in any way in this window. It must be stored on your hard drive. The two following pages explain how to import from your browser.

IMPORTING WITH INTERNET EXPLORER

The method of importing pages from the web to your own machine varies according to which browser you use. Here the methods for the two most popular browsers are given. The section below looks at how to use Internet Explorer to import a page.

1 IMPORTING A PAGE FROM THE WEB

● Find a web page that interests you.

● Go to the **Edit** menu on the toolbar and choose **Select All**. All the text and graphics on the page will be highlighted.

2 SAVING THE PAGE

● Next, go to **File** on the Menu bar and select **Save As**.

● You will be offered the chance to save the page in in a location of your choice. For this example, we have chosen the **My Documents** folder. It is not important where you save the page as long as you remember where it is, and that you save all other parts of the page in the same location.

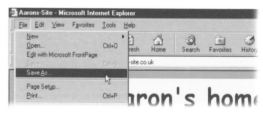

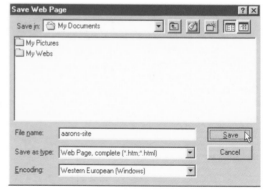

IMPORTING WITH NETSCAPE NAVIGATOR

If you are using Netscape Navigator, you have to import the individual files, such as images, separately. Check that all the graphics you want have been saved before logging off, or blank sections will appear when you look at the page locally.

1 SAVING THE PAGE

● Place the cursor on a page that you want to save and right-click once.
● A pop-up menu appears. Select the **Save Page As** option.

● You will be offered the chance to save the page in a Netscape folder. It will be easier to find if you save the page in your **My Documents** folder.
● However, it is not important where you save the page, as long as you keep all other elements of the page together.

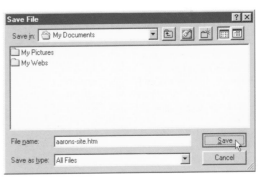

2 IMPORTING GRAPHICS

● If the page that you chose to import contains images or other graphics, you will find that you need to import each these elements individually because they are separate files. This may not be apparent when you view the page with a web connection open, but with a web connection closed, some of the images will not appear.

● Choose the graphic that you want to save.

● With your cursor on the graphic, right-click on the image and choose the **Save As** option. Save the image in the same folder in which the page was saved.

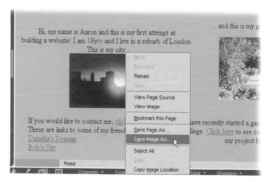

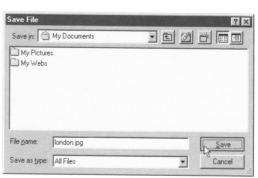

IMAGE FILE NAMES

You may find that when you view the local page in your browser, the images you imported are still not appearing. Usually this is a problem with the full path name of the image. Check that you have saved the image in the same folder as the main page, and that you have saved it under the same name as the image first had when you imported it. Now check how the name of the image appears in the reference in the HTML code of the page: `<img src="…">`. If there is anything more than the name that you have just saved into the folder, delete the extra details. For example, you have saved the image **Edinburgh.jpg** but the full tag in the page reads: `<img src="Images/ Edinburgh.jpg">`, so delete the reference to **Images/**. It should now work as expected.

EDITING THE CODE

The best way of learning about how a page is made up is to unmake it, being careful to tackle only a small stage at any given time. Sometimes you may be exploring tiny steps – like removing a single tag from a table. Occasionally you will take out the whole table, or a section of the page ⌐, and then put it back. By continuing like this throughout a page of source code, you will gain a good understanding of its functions. Follow the steps below in such a way that all your deletions are reversible, but you can also see what effect each step has in the browser.

1 OPENING THE PAGE

● Open the saved page from the **My Documents** folder, by double-clicking on it.

● You are now ready to switch between your Notepad text editor and your browser to see what happens when you work with text ⌐.

● Keep the browser window open while you move on to the next step.

2 OPENING NOTEPAD

● Find your Notepad editor by going to the **Start** menu, selecting **Programs**, then selecting **Accessories**, and clicking on **Notepad**.

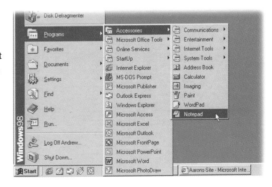

3 OPENING A PAGE

● Notepad opens onscreen. Go to the **File** menu on the Notepad Menu bar and click on **Open**.

● Change the **Files of type** from **Text Documents** to **All Files (*.*)**.

● Go to the folder in which you have saved your imported web pages, such as **My Documents**, or the directory you have chosen.

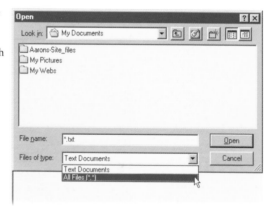

● Click on the name of the page you want to work with and click on **Open**.

Here is the file that we saved earlier.

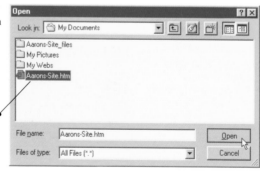

● You can now see the
HTML code in Notepad,
and it is possible to edit it
here.

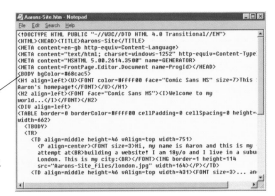

*Here is the HTML code. At
first glance it looks a little
confusing, but with time and
practice, enhancing and
adapting your website can
become easy using this method.*

4 CUTTING THE CODE

● Highlight a section of
code with your mouse (for
example, all the code
between the opening set of
tags for a table: **<table>**
and the closing set:
<\table>).
● Then go to the **Edit**
menu and select **Cut**.

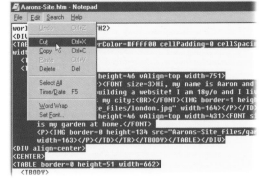

● Save the document by
going to the **File** menu and
selecting **Save**.
● Return to the browser.

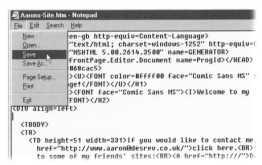

TOGGLING

Toggling is the process of switching between programs without having to close either, or having to use the mouse. It is in fact a very quick way of working.

To toggle, have two programs open on your computer. Of course you could make both windows very small, but this is awkward to use and view. Instead, hold down the [Alt] key on your keyboard and simultaneously press the [Tab⇆] key. By keeping the [Alt] key pressed and tapping the [Tab⇆] key you can have the options of switching between programs very quickly.

5 REFRESHING THE PAGE

● In the browser, press the **Refresh** button (or **Reload** in Netscape) and note carefully which section (if any) has disappeared.

Cutting and pasting

The method of cutting and pasting above is especially good for exploring sites containing complex code, mysterious devices, and new tricks. Understand these and you can use similar effects yourself.

UNNECESSARY CODE

You will notice, when you are working through the source code for some of your own pages, that HTML editors, such as FrontPage, introduce small pieces of code that are unnecessary. These can be deleted when you are sure that they offer nothing to the page. Follow the steps shown here for checking how sections look after removing parts of the page that are described below and delete anything that is not earning its keep.

● In this instance, as we deleted the code that related to the table (step 4) on our site, the table and all its contents have disappeared.

The table and images within it have disappeared.

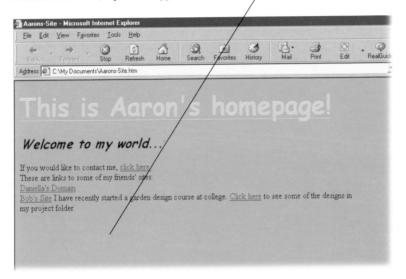

6 REPLACING THE CODE

● Return to the text by pressing Alt and Tab⇄ again to toggle.

● Now replace the section by going to the **Edit** menu and selecting **Paste**. Do not move around in the text or you will replace it in the wrong section.

● Save the document.

● Repeat these stages until you feel that you know the piece of code that controls each part of the page and its particular functions.

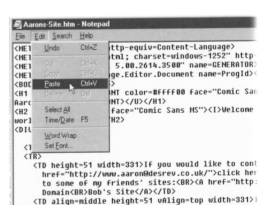

FINDING INSPIRATION IN OTHERS' CODE

There is a fine line between seeking inspiration and stealing. Some sites are copyright-free, some require you to acknowledge the author of images or sections of the page you have borrowed. In other cases, you will be well advised – having explored the site and learned how effects are created – to make sure that anything you write as a consequence is your own work (see Copyright opposite). Of course, if the code belongs to a friend of yours, then you can always ask nicely. The following illustration shows how Aaron (whose site you saw first in chapter three) uses his friend Daniella's code to improve the organization of his site.

1 GAINING PERMISSION

● Aaron calls Daniella to ask to use some material from her site, and she gives her permission.
● Aaron imports Daniella's home page into his computer, using Internet Explorer. He calls it **Daniella's.htm** and saves it in his **My Documents** folder.

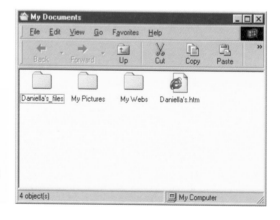

Sources of material
Some sites encourage you to reuse their materials. Alternatively, try searching the web for archives of icons and other graphics.

2 EXTRACTING THE CODE

● After opening the imported page in Notepad, Aaron explores Daniella's use of a table inside another table 🗎.

● Deciding that using her code is going to be a simpler way of getting it just right, rather than starting from scratch, Aaron cuts the section from the first <**table**> tag to the last </**table**> tag on the page.

● *Highlighted table code.*

COPYRIGHT

Copyright is designed primarily to protect the rights of the creator of the content. At the moment, copyright applies to a majority of material produced for, or displayed on, the web. The terms of copyright and intellectual property rights are under review worldwide to ensure that all types of digital material are protected. It is illegal to breach copyright by downloading images unless you have express permission to do so from the copyright holder. You may not reproduce work of any kind on your site unless the material is copyright-free or you have express permission. If in doubt, apply to the copyright holder – the webmaster of the site, in the first instance – or leave well enough alone.

---

3 INSERTING THE CODE

● He opens his own page in Notepad.

● Choosing the point in his page where he wants to use Daniella's device, he pastes the section of her code into his page.

Aaron inserts the text, which he has taken from Daniella's site, into his text at this point.

```
Aarons-Site - Notepad
File  Edit  Search  Help
  <TBODY>
  <TR>
    <TD height=51 width=331>If you would like to
      href="http://www.aaron@desrev.co.uk/">cli
      to some of my friends' sites:<BR><A href='
      Domain<BR>Bob's Site</A></TD>
    <TD align=middle height=51 vAlign=top width
      garden design course at college. <A href='
      here</A> to see some of the designs in <B
folder.</TD></TR></TBODY></TABLE></CENTER></DIV

<TABLE bgColor=#9999ff border=1 borderColor=#00
borderColorLight=#000080 cols=1 height=57 width
  <TBODY>
  <TR>
    <TD bgColor=#9999ff borderColor=#000080 bor
      borderColorLight=#000080 height=51 width=669
      <TABLE bgColor=#9999ff border=1 borderCol
      borderColorDark=#000080 borderColorLight=
      width=669 NOSAVE>
        <TBODY>
        <TR>
          <TD align=middle borderColor=#000080
```

4 EDITING THE CODE

● He changes the name of the image file in one cell of the table to that of one of his own images.

*Aaron types in the name of the new image, **me.jpg**, and the location, **Aarons-Site_files**.*

```
://www.daniellas-domain.com/repository/pdf/
fff face=Arial size=2>Click here to downloa
rite poem by Shakespeare! </FONT></A><

ddle borderColor=#000080 borderColorDark=#0
ight=#000080 height=96 vAlign=center width=
eight=177 src="Aarons-Site_files/me.jpg"

ddle borderColor=#000080 borderColorDark=#0
ight=#000080 height=96 vAlign=top width=96>
fff face=Arial size=2>Likes</FONT>

=left><FONT color=#ffffff face=Arial size=2

=left><FONT color=#ffffff face=Arial size=2
ONT> </P>
```

● Aaron moves further down the text to find the place where he can change the text in the cell above his new photograph.

He types in the new text.

```
<tr>
<td height="51" width="669" bordercolor="#000080" bgc
<table BORDER="1" COLS=4 WIDTH="669" BGCOLOR="#9999FF"
<tr>
<td height="41" width="192" valign="middle" align="cen
  Click here to view my family tree</font></a></td>

<td height="41" width="192" colspan="2" valign="middle
  likes and dislikes </font></td>

<td height="41" width="192" valign="middle" align="ce
```

5 CHANGING THE LINK REFERENCE

● He changes the link referenced in the cell to a site that he wants to connect the page to.

Aaron replaces the link to Daniella's page with one of his own.

```
likes </FONT></TD>
lign=middle borderColor=#000080 borderColorDark=#0000
rColorLight=#000080 height=41 vAlign=center width=192
align=center><A
f="http://www.aarons-site.co.uk/cdrive/pdf/tree.pdf">
or=#ffffff face=Arial size=2>Click here to download a

lign=middle borderColor=#000080 borderColorDark=#0000
rColorLight=#000080 height=96 vAlign=center width=192
der=0 height=177 src="Aarons-Site_files/me.jpg"
```

● He then views his revised page in the browser to check that the new code is working correctly.

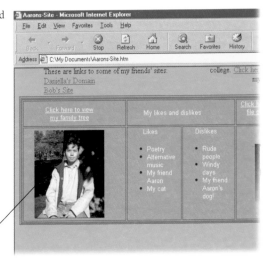

The table now shows Aaron's photograph in place of Daniella's.

LOOKING FOR BUGS IN YOUR PAGE

You can now use the method described to see what has happened in any pages that you have constructed. If something is not working as it should, having a good look at the code, and experimenting with it may well provide the answer. Open your web pages in Notepad and cut out tags or lines until the culprit reveals itself. As everyone's problems are different, there is no particular guidance that can be given. It simply takes patience. Understanding the underlying code will give you more control. However, there are some common mistakes.

1 CHECKING THE IMAGE

● Here is an example of a broken image.
● The photo of London's skyline has not appeared when the site has been brought up by the visitor because the browser can't locate the image. Therefore an empty box is displayed onscreen.

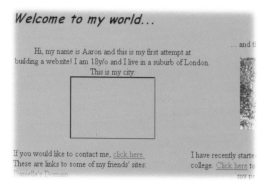

● To find the problem, open the image by typing its file name into the address box of your browser.
● The image will either open in the browser, or in an image-editing program.
● If it appears without any glitches then the problem is with the link to the web page, rather than the image itself.

2 CHECKING THE ADDRESS

● To find out what is wrong with the link between the image file and the page it should be displayed in, check the address of the image file in Notepad.

● It is possible that the address is wrong or part of the image tag has been deleted.

```
   width="662" height="46" cellspacing="0"

51" height="46" align="center" valign="top
center"><font size="3">Hi, my name is Aaro
mpt at<br>
  website!
  and I live in a suburb of London. This is
g border="1" src="London.jpg" width="164"

31" height="46" align="center" valign="top

  garden at home </font>
rder="0" src="garden.jpg" width="163" heigh
```

Image file address seen in Notepad.

3 CHECKING THE FILE NAME

● If there is no problem with the address or the tag, check that the name in the image tag is the same as that of the image in your local folder – it must be the same in all details.

● In this instance, the problem came from the word London having a capital L. You must check whether the image name is spelled out in capitals or in lower case letters – so that all browsers recognize them as the same.

● In this case, you can either change the name of the file or change the coding in the HTML so that they match each other.

● The same technique can be applied to links that fail to connect other pages or sites.

The image's file name.

C:\My Documents\Aarons-Site_files

File Edit View Go Favorites Help

Back Forward Up Cut Copy Paste

Address C:\My Documents\Aarons-Site_files

Aarons-Site.htm   garden.jpg   london.jpg

3 object(s)   My Computer

USING NEW CODE

HTML is not a static language. It has been in a state of continuous development ever since it was first introduced. Maintaining compatibility with this development is vital. When a new version of HTML is introduced, new versions of browsers have to be developed to handle the new features as pages in the new format are put on the web. But this implies that the new browsers have to work with the older versions of HTML, and also all the old browsers have to deal gracefully with the pages in the new format. Browsers have to be very tolerant and ignore anything that they don't understand. It may be some time before the next version of HTML is released, but when it comes, your HTML editor will not support the latest tags. It is not always a good idea to use new tags as soon as they are launched because most people's browsers will not yet recognize them, and they will be ignored. On the other hand, it is fun to explore the potential that they will offer.

WORLD WIDE WEB CONSORTIUM

● This process of evolution is driven and overseen by the World Wide Web Consortium (W3C). Their web pages at **http://www. w3.org/** are essential reading for anyone at all involved in web development.

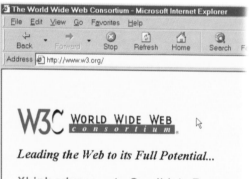

FLEXIBLE XML

HTML can't really be extended much further – it is already a very complex language. Also, it provides us with only a single, comparatively inflexible document type. A new approach is needed to support the future of the web, and XML provides this flexibility. XML is a language used to define mark-up languages. It allows you to define your own mark-up language appropriate for dealing with your own structured data.

XHTML

The next generation of HTML is a version that is compatible with XML, ready for the range of devices that will soon support internet links, such as mobile phones and microwaves. XML specifies the function of the information on the site rather than how the particular function is interpreted. What that means is it describes that, for example, a form that collects a first name is being used, but not the size or look of the form. XHTML functions just like HTML 4, but is more specific. For full details of how to make your HTML comply with XML, visit the W3C pages about XHTML: www.w3.org.

HTML 3.2 (1997)
HTML 4.0 (1997)
HTML 4.01 (1999)
XHTML 1.0 (2000)

```
                    "DTD/xhtml1-transitional.dtd">
        <!DOCTYPE html
            PUBLIC "-//W3C//DTD XHTML 1.0 Frameset//EN"
            "DTD/xhtml1-frameset.dtd">
```

Here is an example of a minimal XHTML document.

```
<?xml version="1.0" encoding="UTF-8"?>
<!DOCTYPE html
    PUBLIC "-//W3C//DTD XHTML 1.0 Strict//EN"
    "DTD/xhtml1-strict.dtd">
<html xmlns="http://www.w3.org/1999/xhtml" xml:lang="en" lang="en">
  <head>
    <title>Virtual Library</title>
  </head>
  <body>
    <p>Moved to <a href="http://vlib.org/">vlib.org</a>.</p>
  </body>
</html>
```

Note that in this example, the XML declaration is included. An XML declaration like the one above is not required in all XML documents. XHTML document authors are strongly encouraged to use XML declarations in all their documents. Such a declaration is required when the character encoding of the document is other than the default UTF-8 or UTF-16.

An example of an XHTML document.

A USER-FRIENDLY SITE

This chapter highlights some of the difficulties encountered when creating a website, and examines issues of incompatibility between different versions of HTML and different browsers.

CREATING MANAGEABLE IMAGES

The previous chapters have introduced many of the facilities provided by HTML, and you will soon become familiar with most of the HTML tags and what they do. However, it takes a little longer to learn how to use HTML effectively.

As you have seen, HTML allows images to be included in web pages. Whenever your pages contain potentially large objects, such as images, you should think about download times. The easiest way to minimize download times is to keep the file size of the images small.

Both JPEG and GIF are highly compressed file formats, and the generally accepted advice is to use JPEG encoding for photographic images and GIF for everything else. It is the browsers rather than HTML that prescribe that GIF or JPEG images are supported.

Defining the image format

To save an image in a JPEG or GIF format, when you have the image open in your image-editing software, go to the **File** menu, choose **Save As**, and select the option for **CompuServe Graphics Interchange** (*.**gif**) or **JPEG** (*.**jpg**) in the file types menu.

LOSING IMAGE QUALITY

GIF compression is "lossless" – in other words, no information about the image is lost when the image is converted into GIF format.

When images are saved in a JPEG format, on the other hand, some information is generally lost. The degree to which information is lost can be controlled by many of the software packages that produce JPEG files. The big advantage of this format is that the file size is much smaller as JPEGs are highly compressed. Since the loss of quality is practically invisible unless extreme compression is used, the compromise of quality for the sake of size is generally worthwhile.

REDUCING IMAGE SIZE

Although the JPEG and GIF formats help to reduce file size, you can reduce the size even further by ensuring that the physical size of your image is not larger than necessary. This can be achieved by resizing your image in an image-manipulation program, such as Paint Shop Pro. We will be using this particular software in the following steps, but almost all image manipulation programs offer the same functions, and can deal with images in both the GIF and JPEG formats.

1 CHECKING THE IMAGE SIZE
● View the HTML code for your image by opening the page in Notepad ⌐.
● By looking at the HTML code you will be able to determine what size your image is being used at – in this case, 148 pixels wide x 177 pixels high.

The pixel dimensions of the image will be listed next to the image name in the HTML code.

```
src="Daniella.jpg" width="148" height="177"></td>
ize="2" color="#FFFFFF">Likes</font>
```

2 OPENING THE IMAGE
● Now open the image file itself in Paint Shop Pro.
● From the **View** menu, select **Image Information** to open the **Current Image Information** window.

⌐33 **Opening notepad**

3 VIEWING IMAGE INFORMATION

● Click on the **Image Information** tab at the top of the window and compare the true dimensions of your image to the HTML code by looking at the values in the **Image** panel.

● You may discover that your image is bigger than required (in this case our image is 311 pixels wide x 373 pixels high).

● Click on the **OK** button to close the window.

The dimensions are shown here. ●

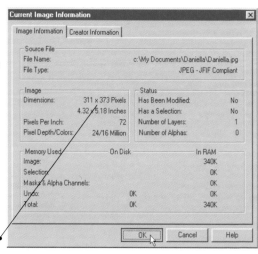

4 RESIZING THE IMAGE

● Select **Resize** from the **Image** menu to open the **Resize** window.

● Resize the image by entering the values that you obtained from the HTML code into the **Width** and **Height** boxes.

● If the values are disproportionate, uncheck the **Maintain aspect ratio** box at the bottom of the window. You will then be able to enter independent values into the **Width** and **Height** boxes.

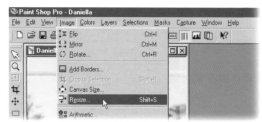

● When you have entered both values, click on the **OK** button.

5 SAVING THE IMAGE

● The image will reduce in size onscreen.

● Select **Save** from the **File** menu to save the changes to your image.

● When you return to view your web page in the browser, you will not see any visible effect on the image, as the HTML instruction to display the image at that particular size has not been changed.

● However, the file size of the image itself will have been significantly reduced, and this will result in a shorter download time.

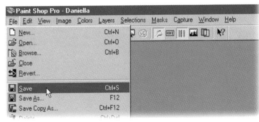

SOURCING IMAGES

Images can be obtained directly from CD-ROM collections (there are many copyright-free image CD-ROMs available), from other web sites, by taking pictures with a digital camera, or by scanning images in. It's a good idea to store the images required by a page on the same computer that is storing the page.

CHECKING THE DISPLAY SIZE

Web pages are viewed on a wide variety of display devices. Browsers do a pretty good job of making the translation from the HTML source code to the display device, but there are many things that the HTML author can do to help. Most of the audience for most web pages use a personal computer/workstation with a conventional color display, but there are still variations, particularly in the sizes and screen resolutions of the displays. Avoid making assumptions about screen size. Try out your web page by resizing your browser window. Use dimensions represented as percentages of screen size rather than pixel numbers wherever possible.

SPECIFYING THE SIZE OF THE PAGE
● If you set your tables and images in pixel sizes, when the browser is resized to be smaller, your visitors will see only the part of the page that fits into their window. Pixels define a fixed space for the elements on the page, which cannot be altered by the user.

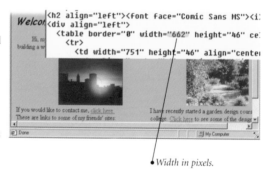

Width in pixels.

MAKING A PAGE THAT RESIZES ITSELF
● On the other hand, if you set the size of these elements in percentage terms, the browser will expand or shrink the tables and images according to the size of the window your visitor has open.

Width as a proportion of screen width. ●

USING BROWSER-SAFE COLORS

Although your computer may be capable of displaying many millions of colors, your HTML should be written to be compatible with as many different computer systems as possible, and some of these will not offer as many colors. "Browser-safe" colors are a set of 216 different colors that can be displayed accurately in all commonly used browsers running on most computer systems.

COLOR DEFINITIONS
● Colors are specified by name (e.g. **purple**) or in the form of a hexadecimal number, such as #FFFFFF (representing white).
● You can find further details of color naming and the browser safe set of colors at **http://www.w3. org/Markup/Guide/Style. html**.

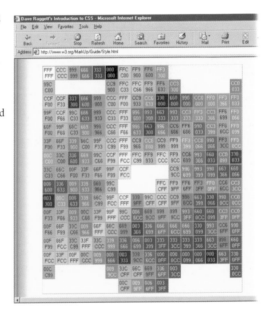

CHOOSING COLORS
● Remember that some of your audience will be color blind. For example, green text on a red background isn't a good choice.

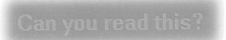

BROWSER INCOMPATIBILITIES

There are some significant differences between the sets of HTML tags accepted by the two most popular browsers, Microsoft Internet Explorer and Netscape Navigator. If you want your website to have a large audience, you must check that your pages can be displayed satisfactorily by both systems.

INTERNET EXPLORER vs NETSCAPE NAVIGATOR

● Differences between the browsers can be a big problem. There are web sites that deliberately use HTML extensions that are only supported by one of the browsers. The only way around this is to make sure that the HTML you write adheres to the W3C HTML standards ⌐.

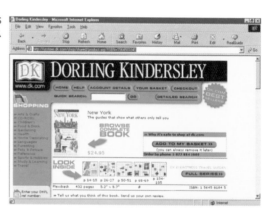

OTHER SYSTEMS

There are also differences between the same browser running under different operating and computer systems (for example, Netscape Navigator running on a PC, a Unix or Linux system, and an Apple Macintosh), but these differences tend to be less awkward and are more likely to be concerned with font availability.

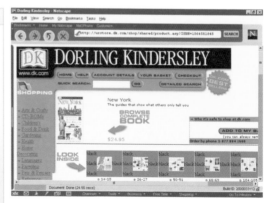

The same page displayed in Microsoft Explorer (top), and Netscape Navigator (bottom). Notice the differences at the bottom of the screen.

CHECKING FOR COMPATIBILITY

To check that your HTML is compliant with a W3C standard, you can find the definition of the standard on the W3C website (**http://www.w3.org/**) and check by hand. This is laborious and prone to error, but it's a good way of developing your HTML coding skills.

A better approach uses a browser called Amaya. This is an HTML browser and editor developed by the W3C, and it is intended to be a reference implementation of HTML. If your pages are displayed correctly using Amaya, then you should have clean, compliant code.

1 OPENING A PAGE IN AMAYA

● Just like any other editing program, open your web page in Amaya by selecting **Open document** from the **File** menu.

● In the **Open Document** window click on the **Browse** button.

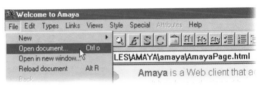

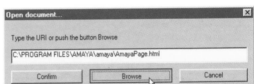

● Locate the web page on your computer, select the file, and click on **Open**.

Obtaining Amaya
You can download Amaya free of charge from **http://www. w3.org/amaya/**, and versions are available for a range of platforms and operating systems.

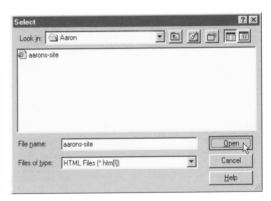

2 VIEWING YOUR PAGE

● Your page will be displayed in the window.
● If your page looks different from the way you expect, then you should think about checking your HTML code for accuracy.
● Remember that, if you wish, you can now use Amaya to edit your page(s).

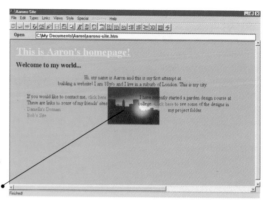

The images on Aaron's page are appearing incorrectly in Amaya.

VALIDATING HTML ON THE WEB

If you want to check pages that have already been published on the web, you can use a validator program provided by the W3C. The program trawls through the code and reports back on any errors detected in the HTML source of the page.

1 OPENING THE VALIDATOR

● Type **http://validator. w3.org/** into the **Address** box of your web browser and press the [Enter ↵] key.
● The **HTML Validation Service** screen will open.

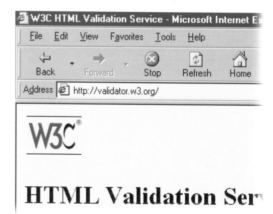

2 ENTERING THE WEB ADDRESS

● Type the address of the page that you wish to be validated into the **Address** box. Remember that, for the pages to be accessible to the validator, they must already be on the web.

● Click on the **Validate this page** button.

Enter the web address here.

W3C®

At
Upload files |

HTML Validation Service

Welcome to the W3C HTML Validation Service. It checks HTML do
XHTML Recommendations and other HTML standards. Recent updat

- XHTML documents are now checked for validity (June 30, 2000)
- Added file upload feature (April 28, 2000)
- more...

Enter the address (URI) of a document you would like to validate:

Address: |www.dk.com
☐ Show source input ☐ Show an outline of this document
☐ Show parse tree ☐ exclude attributes from the parse tree
| Validate this page | Reset this form |

3 VIEWING THE RESULTS

● After a few moments, the results will be returned, and any errors that have been found in your HTML code will be indicated in a list.

Other checking tools
The W3C also provides a stand-alone tool called **Tidy** for checking HTML. See **http://www. w3.org/People/Raggett/ tidy/**

W3C® **HTML Validation Servic**

Document Checked

- URI: http://www.dk.com/ I was redirected to <URI:http://www
- Server: Microsoft-IIS/4.0
- Content length: 1079
- Character encoding: unknown
- Document type: HTML 4.0 Transitional

Below are the results of attempting to parse this document with an SGM

- Line 1, column 1:

  <html>
  ^

  Error: Miss   CTYPE declaration at start of document (exp

- Line 17, column 102:

PROMOTING YOUR SITE

You have built a website and are ready to go public. How public can you go? The principal steps to take are to embed your site on the web, and then to promote it.

EMBEDDING YOUR SITE ON THE WEB

You may have already published a site, but if you want to exploit the web-like nature of the web, you can do a whole lot more than just make your site available. The web is what is known as "pull" technology – in other words, people have to come to you to see your content, unlike something like email where you send it out to others (this is known as "push" technology). The problem with having to "pull" people to you is that they have to know you are there first.

PROMOTING YOUR SITE

Once you have a site, you can say anything that you want to about yourself, your organization, or your interests. When you first launch the site onto the web, you may want to send around an email telling colleagues or friends about it and where to find it. Put the address (the URL) into your email signature. Get the address printed on any stationery you use – your letterhead and your card. If you belong to any newsgroups, politely alert the members to the content that you think they will find interesting. Take out an ad in a topical magazine if you wish to attract a particular group of people to it.

WORD OF MOUTH

Refer people to your site: potential employers or business partners, and new acquaintances. You can use it to display a map to your house for a party and put the page address on the invitations. Once you have a site, remember to promote it at all times – word of mouth is a powerful way to attract people to your creation.

REGISTERING YOUR SITE WITH SEARCH ENGINES

Search engines send out agents to collect new pages, but you can speed the process up by registering your site with each engine. Details of how to do so are published on each search engine – they differ.

PROMOTION THROUGH THE WEB

There are also ways of using the web to full advantage in promoting your site. Web pages show only part of the information on them to visitors. As you have just seen, HTML tags are invisible. So is the meta-data that is written into the Head of the HTML code. Only words put into the Body section appear on the page.

HOW META-DATA HELPS TO PROMOTE YOUR PAGE

● Many of the search engines collect and classify pages with software that trawls the web for new sites. The title and keywords on your pages helps the search engine to decide when to display your pages in answer to people's requests.

● Some pages contain the same keywords repeated many times over to increase the likelihood that certain of the search engines will display them in the first 10 choices shown to visitors.

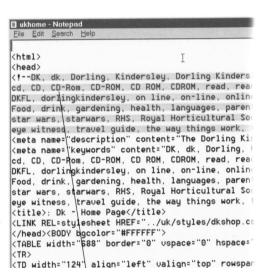

```
🗒 ukhome - Notepad
File  Edit  Search  Help

<html>
<head>
<!--DK, dk, Dorling, Kindersley, Dorling Kinders
cd, CD, CD-Rom, CD-ROM, CD ROM, CDROM, read, rea
DKFL, dorlingkindersley, on line, on-line, onlin
Food, drink, gardening, health, languages, paren
star wars, starwars, RHS, Royal Horticultural So
eye witness, travel guide, the way things work,
<meta name="description" content="The Dorling Ki
<meta name="keywords" content="DK, dk, Dorling, 
cd, CD, CD-Rom, CD-ROM, CD ROM, CDROM, read, rea
DKFL, dorlingkindersley, on line, on-line, onlin
Food, drink, gardening, health, languages, paren
star wars, starwars, RHS, Royal Horticultural So
eye witness, travel guide, the way things work, 
<title>: Dk - Home Page</title>
<LINK REL=stylesheet HREF="../uk/styles/dkshop.c
</head><BODY bgcolor="#FFFFFF">
<TABLE width="688" border="0" vspace="0" hspace=
<TR>
<TD width="124" align="left" valign="top" rowspan
<TD align="left" valign="top"><IMG name="image3"
```

The character string <!-- introduces a comment in HTML. Text between <!-- and --> is ignored by the browser. When writing HTML by hand, comments can be useful to future readers of your code (including yourself). Some search engines may use the text contained in comments when creating their index of web pages. This particular page mentions the keywords both as comments and as meta-data.

1 CREATING META-DATA

● Even without your intervention, your HTML editor will have written things into the <head> section of the page, which generally are superfluous.

● Within the same <head> section, you may have added a page title.

● There is also space for the creation of keywords – both these and page titles can be useful promotional devices.

```
🗊 aarons-site - Notepad                                                    _ 🗗 ✕
File  Edit  Search  Help
<html>

<head>
<meta http-equiv="Content-Language" content="en-gb">
<meta http-equiv="Content-Type" content="text/html; charset=windows-1252">
<meta name="GENERATOR" content="Microsoft FrontPage 4.0">
<meta name="ProgId" content="FrontPage.Editor.Document">
<title>Aarons-Site</title>
</head>

<body bgcolor="#68CAC5">

<h1 align="left"><u><font face="Comic Sans MS" size="7" color="#FFFF00">This is Aaron's
homepage!</font></u></h1>
<h2 align="left"><font face="Comic Sans MS"><i>Welcome to my world...</i></font></h2>
<div align="left">
  <table border="0" width="662" height="46" cellspacing="0" cellpadding="0" bordercolor="#FFFF00"
    <tr>
      <td width="751" height="46" align="center" valign="top">
        <p align="center"><font size="3">Hi, my name is Aaron and this is my
        first attempt at<br>
        building a website!
        I am 18y/o and I live in a suburb of London. This is my city:<br>
        </font><img border="1" src="london.jpg" width="164" height="114"></p>
      </td>
      <td width="431" height="46" align="center" valign="top"><font size="3">...
      and
      this is my garden at home.</font>
      <p><img border="0" src="garden.jpg" width="163" height="134"></td>
    </tr>
  </table>
</div>
```

● The title of the page appears within the <head> section.

● The rest of the meta-data between the <head> tags has been automatically included by the HTML editor, and can be deleted if you wish.

RECIPROCAL LINKS

You can link from your site to as many other sites as you like. However, this is no help in bringing people into your site, it just promotes the sites you link to. One way around this is to get in touch with sites that you are thinking of making a link to on your site and asking them if they would consider making a link to your site. Some sites have no external links, or careful policies about to whom they link, but many site producers are open to suggestion. Contact details for the person in charge of the site are usually displayed on the site somewhere, and this is a good place to start.

CHOOSING KEYWORDS

● Think about how you find pages of interest using a search engine. Which keywords work well for you?

● You can look at meta-data when you use your browser to look at a web page's source code 🗂, so why not look at the meta-data of some web pages at the top of a search list?

● Choose some words that sum up the content of your website. Use the same words for each page, or different ones, depending on the topic.

2 ENTERING KEYWORDS

● To add keywords to your page, you need to type the following code into the <head> section at the top of the page, replacing the words specific to Aaron's site with some of your own:

<meta name = "Keywords" content = "Aaron, aaron, garden, gardens,

gardening, garden design">

● Alternatively, you can add a list of keywords in the empty field provided by your HTML editor.

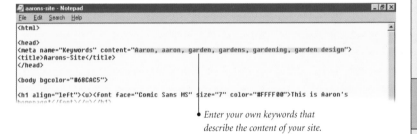

● *Enter your own keywords that describe the content of your site.*

RECIPROCAL ADS

One step up from reciprocal links are reciprocal ads. Ads on websites are usually in the shape of small banners or other graphical devices that link through to the site being advertised. The ads are designed by the person who wants to advertise (or someone working for you) so that the image style is consistent with the design of the site that the ad leads to, and different from the site on which it appears. It is easy to send over the image for your ad to the other site's developer by attaching it to an email. You may want to agree on which page the ad is to appear. Once you have received theirs, you can place it somewhere on the page you agreed on and link it to the other site.

OTHER PAGE ELEMENTS

There are many components to websites beyond HTML,
and this chapter introduces them. Knowing what each can do
gives you more power in designing your pages.

OTHER FILES SUPPORTED IN WEBSITES

The most obvious additional file type to appear among the HTML of the page is the image file ⌐. You will already have worked with GIF or JPEG images, and these are handled automatically by the browser if you put a call in your pages to an image file using the image tag: <img>.

However, websites can contain or refer to files of many different types, and most commonly used browsers (if correctly configured) will deal with these different file types appropriately. As new software applications are introduced, browsers can be configured to handle the new file types.

MULTIMEDIA

● Web pages often contain links to data in a variety of multimedia formats. For example, in this extract from a NASA page, video and audio files can be loaded and played on the user's computer.

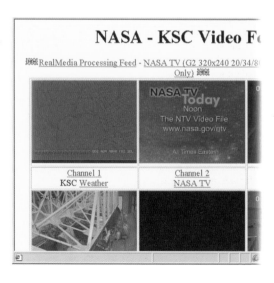

ADOBE ACROBAT

● Another commonly used file type is the portable document format (pdf) of Adobe Acrobat. This is a way of making documents accessible on the web exactly as you wish them to appear. The browser is configured to launch the Acrobat software as soon as it recognizes a pdf file. If your visitors do not have Acrobat on their machine, they can download it from the web.

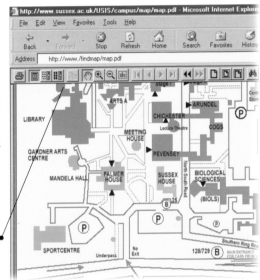

This map is a pdf file, and it is seen displayed in the Adobe Acrobat window, which has opened on top of the browser.

FILES THAT NEED PLUG-INS

● Browsers cope with many of the new file types used on websites (such as audio, animation, and video files) by launching the required software, but the software must be on the visitor's computer. If it is not, the browser can often find the correct plug-in software on the web. To get an idea of the range of plug-ins available, take a look at Netscape's plug-in pages at **http://home. netscape. com/plugins/**.

MAKING PAGES INTERACTIVE

HTML can incorporate many features, but apart from using the "mailto" feature to link email forms into the page ⌐, it cannot supply any interaction between your visitors and the pages they are looking at, or send information back to you. To do more than provide an email link, you will need to understand a little basic programming. The information in the following pages will give you an idea of what is taking place in the more complex languages of the web. To use them yourself, you will need to become more familiar with their structure, just as you have done with HTML. If you learn how to write applications in other languages, you will have the means to make sites interactive and make other changes to the look of your pages. Because each language is rather complex, these pages only offer a general introduction to what they can do, together with some examples.

RUNNING PROGRAMS WITHIN THE PAGE

● There are three ways in which websites manage applications. There are application instructions that form part of the page, and appear in the source code as commands that can be cut and pasted ⌐. This is the nature of JavaScript.

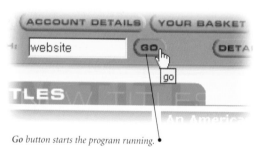

Go button starts the program running. ●

● Then there are applications that are "called" in the text, in the same way as other files. You will only see references to the call, not the entire code that makes the application work. Programs written in Java and Perl ⌐ lie behind these. Search boxes are a good example. When you fill in the box and click on **Go**, a program runs at the server, not on your machine.

● Result of the search program.

JAVASCRIPT

JavaScript is a language closely modeled on Java ⌐. It is a language that is used to control the operation of the browser, allowing the appearance of displayed pages to be specified and pages to be generated dynamically. Java responds to the user's actions, producing, for example, pop up windows and rollovers (when images or words change as website visitors move their cursor over them). It also allows programs to be executed on the server as well as on the client, providing an alternative to the CGI facility using Perl. Many pages include sections written in JavaScript. The JavaScript program is included in the HTML file as an identifiable tagged section.

FINDING JAVASCRIPT

● A good way of starting to work with JavaScript is by looking at web pages. The JavaScript contained in them is visible when the source code of the page is downloaded. Sites such as **http://www.javascript.com/** contain many examples of JavaScript that could be useful for inclusion in your web pages.

SHOOT 'EM UP

● JavaScript can be used for a wide range of applications. In this example (**http://javascript. internet.com/games/rocket -blaster.html**), a simple rocket shooting game has been implemented in JavaScript.

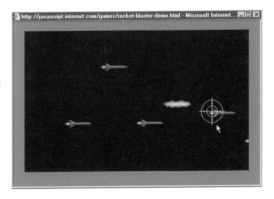

JAVA

Java is used in all kinds of software, but it is particularly useful on the web because it is capable of performing in the same way regardless of what type of computer or browser it is working on – a flexibility that most software code doesn't possess.

HOW JAVA RUNS

● When a call to a Java "applet" – a small application – is made in a web page, the browser downloads a file containing the applet code. This is opened in the Java Virtual Machine in your browser, creating an environment in which Java code can run on your machine without interfering with anything that already exists in your files. This is important for security. Unfamiliar files are imported when Java code is called, and this system keeps everything separate. Once the applet is ready to use, it can change the page immediately without reference to the server on which the pages are stored.

● Java has many uses, but often without consideration for the visitor who has to wait for the file with the code to download from the site being visited, as well as the page in which the applet will perform.

```
HelloWorld.txt - Notepad
File  Edit  Search  Help
<HTML>
 <HEAD>
 <TITLE> A Simple Program </TITLE>
 </HEAD>

 <BODY>

 Here is the output of my program:
 <APPLET CODE="HelloWorld.class" WIDTH=200 HEIGHT=100>
 </APPLET>
 </BODY>
</HTML>
```

This piece of HTML "calls" up the Java applet.

A VERY SIMPLE JAVA PROGRAM

Java "applets" reside on the server where the web page is stored. The "call" embedded in the HTML of the web page (shown above) causes the applet shown here to be downloaded and run.

```
import java.applet.Applet; import java.awt.Graphics;
public class HelloWorld extends Applet {
    public void paint(Graphics g) {
        g.drawOval(80, 50, 40, 40);
        g.drawString("Hello world!", 50, 25);
    }
}
```

GETTING STARTED

● Not surprisingly, the web contains a vast amount of information on Java – just try searching for the word **Java** using a web search engine. A helpful way to start writing Java applets is to look at the tutorial at **http://java.sun. com/docs/books/tutorial/ getStarted/cupojava/win32. html**. This site gives a step-by-step introduction to the implementation of a simple Java applet and provides pointers to further Java resources. Tutorials for Unix and Macintosh users are also available at the same website.

Trail: Getting Started
Lesson: Your First Cup of Java

Your First Cup of Java (for Win32)

Detailed Instructions
for Your First Program

The following instructions will help you w॒
Java program. These instructions are for u
Win32 platforms, which include Windows
Windows 95, and Windows NT.

1. A Checklist

2. Creating Your First Appl
  a. Create a Java Source File
  b. Compile the Source File
  c. Run the Program

3. Creating Your First Applet

4. Where to Go from Here

JAVA RESOURCES

● There are many sites offering free Java applets for you to examine and include in your web pages. For example, **http://java.sun. com/openstudio/index. html** contains many applets that may be of direct use for your web pages. Have a careful look at the Java code and you will learn a lot about programming in Java, customizing existing applets, and developing new applets to your precise specifications.

A-Z Index • [   ] (Search)

THE SOURCE FOR JAVA™ TECHNOLOGY
java.sun.com

FREEBIE APPLETS YOU CAN USE

Open Studio | Adding Applets | Resources
What Is Java™ Technology | Tutorial | Java Developer Connection™ Program

The applets below are available for use on your websites. All of the necessary class files and example HTML markup are contained in a single zip file. The HTML markup necessary to use the applets is explained in detail on a separate page for each applet. For more generic instruction in the use of applets start with our beginner's guide. For anyone interested in the Java™ programming language, the source files are also included in the same zip file.

PERL

The Common Gateway Interface (CGI) is another way of adding functions to a site. The program that manipulates the page is stored on the site's server and is only used if a visitor and sends some data by hitting the Send or Submit button. The language most frequently used is Perl. Because the programs are stored on the producer's server, it is also a secure way of handling the transfer of data. Because Perl code has to be mounted on the server storing the pages, if you do not have your own server, you will need to ask your Internet Service Provider for permission. The website **cgi-lib.berkeley.edu/** is an excellent source of Perl code and information about Perl.

 The cgi-lib.pl Home Page

Intro / Documentation / Examples / Books

cgi-lib.pl

The **cgi-lib.pl** library has become the *de facto* standard library for creating Common Gateway Interface (CGI) scripts in Perl language. Welcome to the official Web site for **cgi-lib.pl**, with the most up-to-date releases of the library.

The cgi-lib.pl library makes CGI scripting in Perl easy enough for anyone to process forms and create dynamic Web cont... The library has the following features:

HOW CGI OPERATES

• The HTML tag <form> in the source code of a website introduces the definition of a form and defines a set of boxes to appear on the browser's screen. This is called a web form, and the user can type information into the boxes.

• The contents of the form (i.e. the fields completed by the user) are then sent back to the server in a standard format.

• The server passes the form contents to a program that decodes the text in the fields and performs predetermined actions depending on the values of these fields.

• The results from this program are expressed in the form of HTML and this code is passed back to the browser. The browser then decodes the HTML and presents the results to the user.

PERL FOR THE TAKING

● This example of Perl is a typical CGI application. It is one of many samples that can be downloaded from the cgi-lib website. This one is a form to collect information from visitors to a website. It checks that the information is in a manageable form, and then stores the data in sections so that it can be processed more easily. The Perl code that creates this form, and which can be downloaded, is shown below.

A simple form example - Microsoft Internet Explorer

File   Edit   View   Favorites   Tools   Help

Back   Forward   Stop   Refresh   Home   Search   Favorites   History

Address http://cgi-lib.berkeley.edu/ex/simple-form.html

This is a sample form which demonstrates the use of the cgi-lib.pl library of rou

Pop Quiz:

What is thy name:

What is thy quest:

What is thy favorite color: chartreuse

What is the weight of a swallow: ⦿ African Swallow or ○ Continental Swall

```perl
@in = split(/[&;]/, $in);
push(@in, @ARGV) if $cmdflag; # add command-line parameters

foreach $i (0 .. $#in) {
  # Convert plus to space
  $in[$i] =~ s/\+/ /g;

  # Split into key and value.
  ($key, $val) = split(/=/, $in[$i], 2); # splits on the first =.

  # Convert %XX from hex numbers to alphanumeric
  $key =~ s/%([A-Fa-f0-9]{2})/pack("c", hex($1))/ge;
```

APPLICATIONS

This facility opens up an enormous range of applications. For example, you can set up a web page that includes a form to ask for name and address details so that further information can be sent. Here, the application program running on the server is simple – it simply has to store the name and address details. Another common example is to allow the entry of keywords to be sent to a search engine – here, the application running on the server has to do more complex work. CGI is, of course, central to the implementation of most e-commerce sites – it acts as the interface to some form of sales database.

FURTHER INFORMATION

The best source of information about the web is, of course, the web itself. Here are some URLs that provide information about the web, HTML, recent developments, and usability.

A SITE DIRECTORY

This section lists a selection of websites covering HTML, markup languages, and usability that will help provide further information on the topics introduced in this book. Try visiting some of these sites to see the wealth of help and advice available. These websites themselves obviously contain further pointers.

HTML

An essential source of up-to-date and definitive information is the World Wide Web Consortium's site.
http://www.w3.org/

This site hosts pages on Amaya
http://www.w3.org/Amaya/

The W3C HTML Validation Service
http://validator.w3.org/

HTML converters
http://www.w3.org/Tools/Filters.html

Tidy
http://www.w3.org/People/Raggett/tidy/

HTML and variants
http://www.w3.org/MarkUp/

This beginner's guide introduces HTML and style sheets too.
http://www.w3.org/MarkUp/Guide/

Another beginner's guide.
http://www.ncsa.uiuc.edu/General/Internet/WWW/HTMLPrimer.html

Information from the Web Design Group
http://www.htmlhelp.com/

An excellent guide to HTML style.
http://info.med.yale.edu/caim/manual/

Quick reference sites
http://bignosebird.com/html.shtml
http://www.willcam.com/cmat/html/crossref.html

OTHER MARKUP LANGUAGES

XML information.
http://www.xml.com/

VRML information, managed by the Web3D consortium.
http://www.web3d.org/vrml/vrml.htm

USABILITY

Formerly part of the National Physical Laboratory, this site offers good advice.
http://www.usability.serco.com/info.html

For some suggestions on how HTML can be used and abused
http://wackyhtml.com/

Another author on web design provides some useful pointers on his site.
http://www.horton.com/

Jakob Nielsen's bimonthly column discusses Web design issues back to '95.
http://www.useit.com/alertbox/index.html

This site pulls together many other sources to bring the latest in news and ideas together.
http://webword.com/index.html

How not to do it... a lesson in what's good from what's bad.
http://www.webpagesthatsuck.com/index.html

The most comprehensive list of usability sites, this offers hundreds of links on all aspects of design and structure.
http://usableweb.com/

OTHER TOOLS

The following are teach yourself Perl websites:
http://www.ebb.org/PickingUpPerl/pickingUpPerl.html http://agora.leeds.ac.uk/Perl/start.html

CGI script library
http://cgi-lib.berkeley.edu/

Java
http://java.sun.com/

JavaScript
http://www.javascript.com/

Acrobat
http://www.adobe.com/

GLOSSARY

APPLET
A small application that runs on a web page, usually written in Java.

APPLICATION
A function that has been added to a website by using a full program, rather than HTML.

BROWSER
Software used to view websites. Internet Explorer and Netscape Navigator are two browsers.

CODE
Any text on the source page that is not shown on the final page in the browser.

COMPRESSION
A system of reducing the size of a computer file, often to make an image faster to download.

DOWNLOAD
Transferring data from one computer to another. Your browser downloads HTML code and graphics to display a page.

EMAIL (ELECTRONIC MAIL)
The system of sending electronic messages between computers.

GIF (GRAPHICS INTERCHANGE FORMAT)
A widely used file format for web-based images.

HTML (HYPERTEXT MARKUP LANGUAGE)
A computer language used to create web pages. HTML consists of a number of tags that describe how a page should be displayed.

INTERNET
The network of interconnected computers that communicate using the TCP/IP protocol.

ISP (INTERNET SERVICE PROVIDER)
A business that provides your connection to the internet.

JAVA
A powerful language that is used on the web for writing programs that control the look or function of the page.

JAVASCRIPT
A language that is used on the web for writing small programs that control the look or function of the page.

JPEG (JOINT PHOTO-GRAPHIC EXPERTS GROUP)
A file format for web-based images, particularly for photographic images.

LINK
A shortcut to another web page or place on the page.

NETWORK
A collection of computers that are linked together.

PATH
The address of a file on a computer system.

PERL
A language that is used extensively on the web for writing interactive components such as forms.

PIXEL
A unit of measurement for computer displays. A display consists of a series of pixels that show images on the screen.

SERVER
A computer with a high-speed connection to the internet that serves up web pages.

SOURCE CODE
The page as the browser sees it, with all the coding visible, as well as text to be displayed in the browser window.

TAG
The marking-up component of HTML. Each tag contains an instruction to the browser about structure or display.

URL (UNIVERSAL RESOURCE LOCATOR)
An address on the internet. You type a URL into your browser to visit a website.

WEB PAGE
A single page on a website that can contain text, images, sound, video, and other elements.

WEBSITE
A collection of web pages that are linked together, by style or theme.

WORLD WIDE WEB
The term used to refer to all the websites on the internet that are linked together to form a global web of information.

INDEX

ACKNOWLEDGMENTS

PUBLISHER'S ACKNOWLEDGMENTS
Dorling Kindersley would like to thank the following
Paul Mattock of APM, Brighton, for commissioned photography.
cgi-lib.berkeley.edu (Copyright Steven E. Brennner). Microsoft Corporation for
permission to reproduce screens from within Microsoft® Internet Explorer.

Every effort has been made to trace the copyright holders.
The publisher apologizes for any unintentional omissions and would be pleased,
in such cases, to place an acknowledgment in future editions of this book.

Microsoft® is a registered trademark of Microsoft Corporation
in the United States and/or other countries.

AUTHORS' ACKNOWLEDGMENTS
Des Watson – to Jonathan.
Ann Light would like to thank Debra, for providing the flat
in which these, and so many other words were written.